Picasso

Pablo Picasso was born in the south of Spain on the shore of the Mediterranean Sea. His father was a painter. One day, Pablo's father noticed that his son was drawing pigeons very well—better than he could draw them himself. Seeing that his son was extremely gifted, Picasso's father let him use all of his brushes, palettes and tubes of paint. Immediately, Picasso began to paint.

The Circus

As a boy, Picasso did not like school very much, but he loved to paint. He drew and painted all the time. He won many art contests in Spain. He also loved the circus. He was fascinated by the jugglers, the tumblers and the clowns. He was interested in the workings of the circus—in the colors, the people, and the travels of the show from one city to the next. Later on, when Picasso's own life was filled with moving from city to city, he remembered the clowns and harlequins and painted them.

Harlequins

Picasso painted harlequins not only because of his interest in the circus, but also because it allowed him to experiment with contrasting colors. The clowns, dressed in elaborate costumes, allowed him to practice painting patterns and to experiment with black and white contrasts.

1. The Clown and the Little Boy
   • Baltimore Museum of Art
2. Paul Dressed up as Pierrot
   • Private Collection
3. Picasso's Son in Harlequin Costume
   • Private Collection
4. Paul Dressed up as Pierrot
   • Musée Picasso, Paris.

Paint, Draw,

Paul on his Donkey • Palais Reale, Milan

Picasso painted all the time. He used different types of paints to create different kinds of paintings. Sometimes he painted with thick oil paints, or thinner gouache paint or even light watercolors. At other times, he made line drawings and etchings. He even did collage using materials like newspapers, found around the house. Using all different types of materials, he created one piece of art after another. Often he made twenty drawings in one morning!

Etch, Collage...

With one single stroke, Picasso drew the curve of this face. Notice the softness, the light shading in the cheeks. He would mold the shapes he wanted. In this picture he may have smeared the paint with his thumb, like caressing the boy's face, to make you feel the plumpness of his cheeks.

It's a Picasso!

On the left: Maya Wearing an Apron • Private Collection
On the right: The Gourmet • National Gallery, Washington

Picasso's paintings are very distinct. Looking at these paintings you can tell right away it's a Picasso. He has a very recognizable style.

Picasso painted not just what he saw, but what he felt.

Over the years, Picasso studied many Spanish painters, including El Greco, Velásquez, and Goya. He also studied the work of his famous contemporaries, Matisse

and Rousseau. These artists influenced his work, but Picasso did not copy them. He wanted to do something unique. He wanted to use colors, forms, composition, and perspective in a way that no one else ever had. He especially focused on movement. He believed that paintings should move in the same way that life moves—all the time. Look at the little girl on the left. Her eyes and her fingers are painted as if they are placed in many different positions— so that it looks like she is in motion.

Fantasy, Life!

Picasso's art style changed many times, but it was always distinct. When he first moved to Paris, Picasso was unhappy. Many of his paintings were blue. A few years later he became happier—he began to enjoy his life in France. Soon, his paintings were filled with red. Many of his pieces expressed fantasy and what the French call *joie de vivre* (enjoyment of life). He later experimented in his paintings with sharp lines and cubical shapes. He created elongated or distorted figures. Some people thought that his new painting style was odd. But, Picasso always did what he wanted and painted what he felt.

When I have no blue, I use red!

Opposite: Paloma, lithography • Private Collection • On the right: Claude Writing • Private Collection

Volume

Rest your hand lightly on your face. Feel the roundness of your cheek. Run your hand under your chin. How would you paint this shape, show this roundness? How would you draw these curves on a flat canvas?

Picasso studied forms. He spent a lot of time studying the shapes and lines of the objects he painted. By doing so many drawings he really understood the lines of his piece. That way, he understood how a face is made: with its bumps and hollows. He built the object one piece at a time. He noticed how all the lines give the portrait depth and life. Observe the splendor and charm of his son Claude's face, the softness of his little hand, all round, like a dove.

P̲ablo Ruiz Blasco Picasso was born in 1881 in Málaga, in the south of Spain. He started drawing at an early age. At sixteen he entered the Royal Academy of Madrid. The entrance examinations lasted one month to allow the applicants time to show the teachers what they could create. But, when Pablo completed

his projects in just one day, he was recognized as a prodigy. At nineteen he went to Paris to try his luck in the art world. Picasso lived on the *Montmartre* Mountain with a community of famous artists.

He had no money and led a bohemian life. He drew and painted day and night, and often visited museums. Picasso looked at everything and sought to understand how other artists worked. He absorbed the ancient arts of Mesopotamia, Egypt, and the Middle Ages. He discovered the *Ballets Russes*, which had

Collage Sheet

1. Music Sheet and Guitar.
Musée National d'Art Moderne Georges Pompidou.
2. Violin and Music Sheet
Musee d'Orsay d'Orsay, Paris.

1. © Photo, Centre Georges Pompidou.

2. © Photo, R.M.N.

Picasso liked to do collages.
He used different kinds of paper, sometimes even
newspaper, to make collages.
Enclosed are six printed sheets for you to use to make collages.
You can also make your own sheets by decorating paper with color,
or using pieces of string, cardboard, and cloth.
Get out your scissors and create!

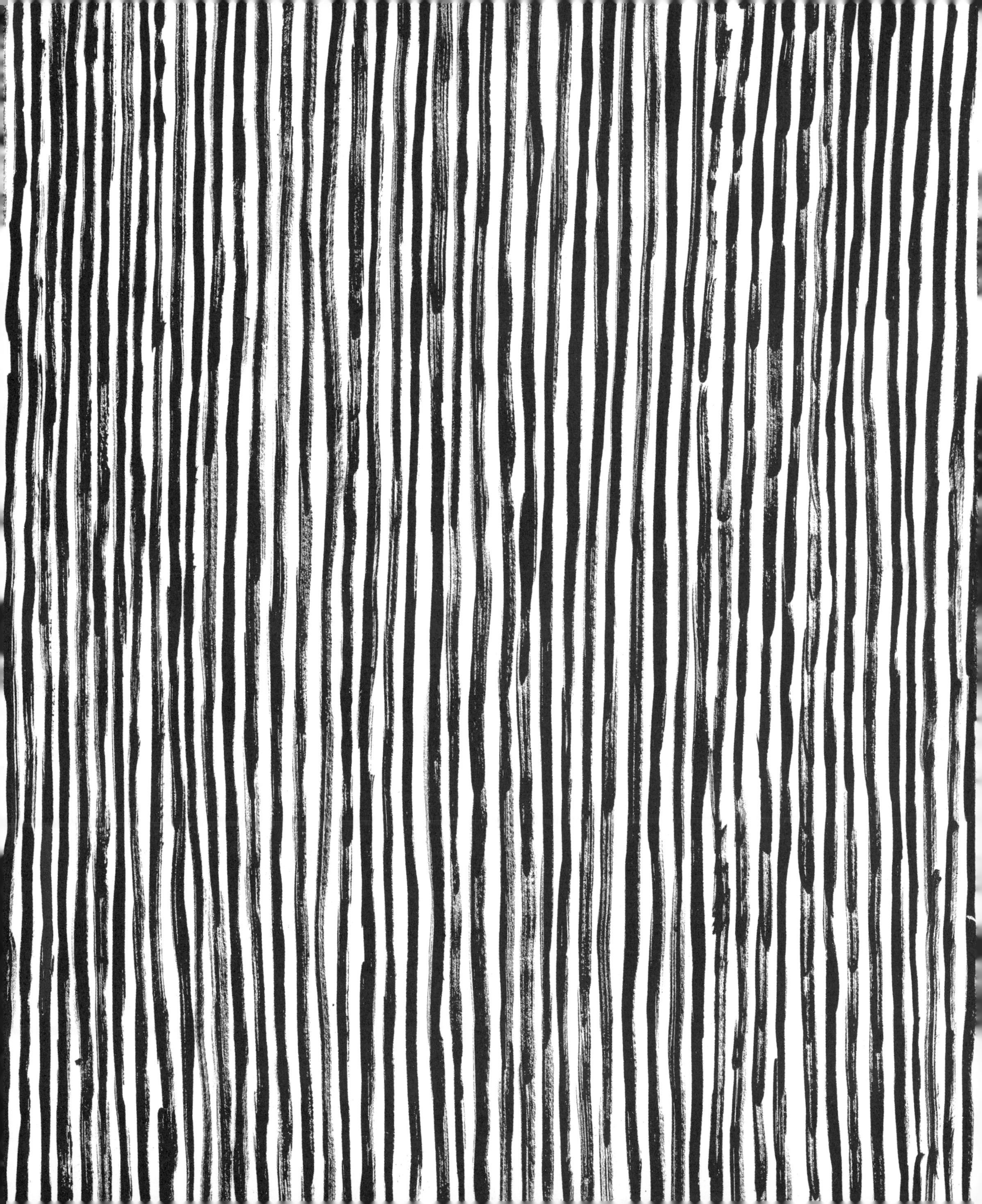